Customs & Traditions
in Britain

UNIVERSITY COLLEGE CHICHESTER LIBRARIES

AUTHOR:
O'HANLON

TITLE:
CUSTOMS

CLASS:
CR 394.26

DATE:
APRIL 2002.

SUBJECT:
CR

D1076909

May Day celebrations have their origins in the Roman festival of Flora, goddess of flowers, which marked the beginning of summer. People would decorate their houses and villages with fresh-cut foliage and flowers gathered at dawn – as they still do today – in the belief that the vegetation spirits thus brought into the community would bring good fortune. The appearance of 'obby 'osses in May is a mystery – most are associated with winter customs – but they are certainly a colourful addition to the festivities.

Unite and unite and let us all unite
For summer is icumen today.
And whither we are going,
we will all unite
In the merry morning of May.
PADSTOW MAY SONG

On a May Morning

◄ *The first maypoles were simply trees decorated with garlands, like the one in this 19th-century illustration.*

Maypoles and May Queens

The original maypoles were freshly felled trees, stripped of their branches, brought into the community, and adorned with garlands and ribbons. The Puritans tried to stamp out this pagan custom but were unsuccessful. The crowning of a child May Queen and the ribbon-plaiting dances commonly associated with maypoles were not introduced until Victorian times. Before then, the May Queen, representing the goddess Flora, was chosen from the prettiest young women of the neighbourhood.

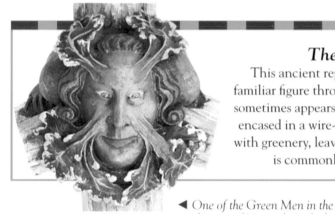

The Green Man

This ancient representation of summer is a familiar figure throughout Europe. In England he sometimes appears as Jack-in-the-Green – a man encased in a wire-netting cage entirely covered with greenery, leaves and flowers – and his image is commonly seen in old churches.

◀ *One of the Green Men in the cloisters of Norwich Cathedral.*

Padstow 'Obby 'Oss Day

In Padstow celebrations begin in the small hours of 1 May, when the Nightsingers tour the town, serenading the occupants of various houses. In the morning, the Blue Ribbon 'Oss is first to appear, followed by the Old 'Oss, and to the sound of massed accordions and an electrifying drumbeat, they swoop and swirl their separate ways through the narrow streets until evening. At intervals, the drums cease and, to the mournful strains of the Day Song, an 'Oss 'dies', only to be revived as the music strikes up again.

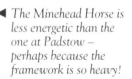

◀ *The Minehead Horse is less energetic than the one at Padstow – perhaps because the framework is so heavy!*

▲ *Old 'Oss and his Teazer in the streets of Padstow, Cornwall.*

The Sailor's Horse, Minehead

On May Day Eve 1722, a dead cow was washed up at Minehead and its tail was cut off, attached to an 'obby 'oss, and used to beat anyone who misbehaved. Whether or not this story is true, an 'obby 'oss with a long rope tail takes to the streets every May Day Eve and, on May Day itself, tours the town and visits Dunster Castle. His attendant 'Gullivers', who appear spasmodically, also have conical masks and once carried tongs and whips.

May Singing, Oxford

May Day in Oxford is welcomed in at sunrise by the choristers of Magdalen College singing hymns and May carols from the top of Magdalen Tower. Despite the early hour, a large crowd always gathers at the bridge below the tower. A peal of bells follows, after which the streets are taken over by morris dancers until life returns to normal at about 9 o'clock.

◀ *May morning singing on Magdalen College Tower, Oxford; an oil painting by William Holman (1827–1910).*

On a May Morning

▶ *The Furry Dance takes place on Flora Day, which is also the feast of St Michael, patron saint of Helston.*

Abbotsbury Garland Day

▼ *Attempts to ban the long-established Abbotsbury Garland Day on the grounds of unlawful begging and time off school have proved unsuccessful.*

Garland Day once marked the opening of the mackerel-fishing season in the Dorset village of Abbotsbury and each boat would sport a garland in its bow. The garlands were first carried to the church for a service and then returned to the boats, after which the fishermen would put to sea and throw the garlands overboard for luck. Although the fishing has long ceased, garlands are still made on Old May Day (13 May) but they are now carried around the village by local children.

Helston Furry Dance

On about 8 May, the Cornish village of Helston blossoms with greenery, flowers and bunting in preparation for the Furry, or Faddy, Dance – one of the oldest examples of a community spring festival dance in Britain. The steps may be simple, but the dance is long, winding through the streets and around or through the houses, led by the Town Band. After the Early Morning Dance, it is the children's turn. Then, at noon, the Principal Dance begins, with behatted ladies in their best frocks accompanied by gentlemen in morning dress. To round off the day, there is a final dance for everyone, including visitors.

Grovely Day, Great Wishford

On the morning of Oak Apple Day (29 May), the people of Great Wishford gather green boughs which they carry to Salisbury Cathedral. Here, a traditional dance is performed by four of the women, after which everyone joins in the cry 'Grovely! Grovely! And all Grovely!' In this way, the villagers re-affirm their rights, granted in 1602, to cut wood in Grovely Forest. Afterwards, the dancers and two men with a banner bearing the Grovely slogan and the words 'Unity is Strength' lead a procession through the village.

Grovely Day dancers with their traditional bundles of oak faggots.

Wishes and Wells

❖

The charming custom of well-dressing is seen almost exclusively in the villages of the Derbyshire Peak District, an area particularly rich in wells and springs. This originally pagan practice of adorning wells with flowers and greenery was absorbed into the early Church – which also appreciated the value of its water supplies. The wells were re-dedicated to some holy personage and, as in the present-day ceremonies, any decoration was performed as an expression of thanksgiving to God rather than to appease any water spirit. Young and old join in the preparation of the well-dressings, which usually have a religious theme and are fashioned on boards of damp clay. Coffee beans or other natural items are pressed into the clay to form the outlines of the picture, and these are then filled with overlapping flower petals and other plant material.

❖

Tissington

Traditionally the first wells of the year to be dressed, at Ascensiontide, are the five at Tissington. This custom is thought to date from 1615, when the wells kept flowing despite a severe drought. The Tissington dressings typically have an inner arch surrounding the picture, and an outer arch with letters and patterns set into a cream or pale green fluorspar background.

▶ *This well-dressing at Coffin Well shows the characteristic arches found in Tissington.*

Tideswell

Well-dressing at Tideswell is comparatively recent and did not begin until after World War II. The village is now noted for the detail and accuracy of its architectural screens, which depict a different cathedral or church every June.

◀ *Well-dressings at Tideswell are noted for their architectural themes.*

▲ *The preparation of a well-dressing is a painstaking process.*

Clootie Wells

In Scotland, some wells – such as Craigie Well, north of Munlochy Bay, and St Mary's Well, by the battlefield of Culloden – are decorated by passers-by with strips of cloth, or 'clooties', representing problems, prayers or wishes. It is traditional to visit the wells before dawn on the first Sunday in May.

Youlgreave

In 1829, when piped water was first laid to the village, the custom of 'tap-dressing' began. The five public taps are still dressed annually each June, around Midsummer Day. Unusually, the clay of the Youlgreave dressings is built up into three-dimensional shapes and colour is applied. Wirksworth, which first received a piped water supply in 1827, observes a similar tradition, although the public taps have long gone.

▶ *The well-dressings at Youlgreave, like this one at Fountain Well, are noted for their artistry.*

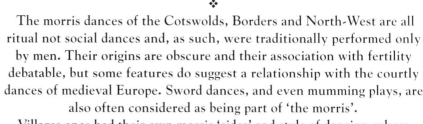

The morris dances of the Cotswolds, Borders and North-West are all ritual not social dances and, as such, were traditionally performed only by men. Their origins are obscure and their association with fertility debatable, but some features do suggest a relationship with the courtly dances of medieval Europe. Sword dances, and even mumming plays, are also often considered as being part of 'the morris'.

Villages once had their own morris 'sides' and style of dancing, whose secrets were passed down from father to son. The loss of so many men in World War I broke this continuity but, fortunately, most dances were rescued by dedicated collectors before they faded into oblivion. Since then, there has been a great revival of interest in the morris and, today, there are male, female and mixed morris sides throughout the country, performing dances from all these areas and not just on high days and holidays.

❖

Morris Dancing

Border Morris

The Border sides seen nowadays are relative newcomers to the present morris scene but records suggest that this style of morris was flourishing in Herefordshire, Worcestershire and Shropshire during the late 19th and early 20th century. Typically, the dancers wear clothes covered with ribbons or strips of cloth and black their faces for disguise. The simple dances generally involve sticks and sometimes tambourines and bones.

◄ *Shropshire Bedlams, who are based in the Border counties, were largely responsible for the current interest in Border morris dancing.*

Cotswold Morris

This gentle stuff of English village greens involves six dancers, commonly dressed in white, with baldricks and bells, sticks and handkerchiefs. The intricate steps and interweaving figures follow patterns that may be centuries old. Indeed, some sides boast an unbroken history of over 400 years, although the original instruments – bagpipes, pipe and tabor, and fiddle – have largely been superseded by concertinas and melodeons.

◄ *Among the Cotswold morris sides, Bampton can probably claim the longest unbroken history.*

Mumming Plays

These folk plays, of which there have been more than 1,000 in Britain, are typically performed around Christmas, Easter or All Souls Night. The plot usually involves a fight to the death between the hero (George) and the villain (Bold Slasher or the Turkish Knight), and the revival of the 'corpse' by the magical potions of the Doctor. The various minor characters provide a touch of humour and also relieve the audience of any spare change!

Morris Dancing

▼ *The high-stepping Ripon City Morris has been performing North-West morris dances since its formation in 1982.*

North-West Morris

What the North-West sides of Lancashire and Cheshire lack in grace is more than compensated for by their sheer presence. You don't argue with a dozen or more burly men in steel-shod clogs dancing along the street, even if they are wearing beads and flowery top-hats – and the women's sides are equally impressive. The sound of clog on concrete or cobblestone is emphasised by the beat of the bass drum, an essential part of the accompanying band. Dances, involving decorated sticks, 'twizzlers' or flexible hoops covered with flowers or ribbons, are executed with an almost military precision and enable the whole side to progress forwards.

Britannia Coconut Dancers

Obviously related to North-West morris are the dances of the 'Nutters', who come from the small village of Britannia, Lancashire, and tour nearby Bacup every Easter Saturday. The dancers all wear 'coconuts' – wooden discs fashioned out of a bobbin top from the cotton-mills – on each knee, in each palm and at the waist, and are kept in order by the 'Whiffler', who carries a whip. Their repertoire includes a processional dance, garland dances, and 'nut' dances, involving complicated figures interspersed with tattoos beaten out on the discs.

▲ *The dances of the Britannia Coconut Dancers, from Bacup, Lancashire, are closely related to those of North-West morris.*

▶ *The High Spen rapper team performing one of the intricate figures of the dance.*

Sword Dancing

Because of the dramatic elements in English sword dancing – the songs, characters, and death and resurrection – sword dancing has sometimes been seen as intermediate between the morris dance and the mumming play. In the dance, each man holds onto the sword of the next man, thus forming a continuous chain, while the whole team executes a series of elaborate, intertwining figures that culminate in the formation of a 'lock'. It is this ingenious linking of swords that enables the 'decapitation' of one of the characters. There are two types of sword dancing: longsword, native to Yorkshire, in which the stiff, flat swords are about a metre long; and rappersword, associated with the miners of Northumberland and Durham, which involves much shorter, flexible steel swords with a handle at each end. The rapperswords may once have been used to scrape the sweat from pit-ponies.

▼ *Flamborough longsword team, bearing the 'lock'.*

▼ *This dancer from the Handsworth side is holding the swords in the 'lock' formation.*

The English monarchy dates from AD927 but the first truly British ruler was James I, who succeeded to the throne in 1603. Given this long history, it is not surprising to find a diversity of time-honoured rituals associated with the reigning monarch, the government and state buildings. While not strictly folk customs, they offer a splendour and pageantry which are seldom found beyond the British Isles.

❖

Pomp and Circumstance

Royal Maundy

On Maundy Thursday, purses of money are distributed to deserving members of a diocese, the numbers of Recipients and Maundy pennies corresponding to the Sovereign's age. As well as a white purse of Maundy coins, each person also receives a red purse containing money in lieu of clothing and provisions. The towels that gird the attendant clergy are a vestige of the original ceremony, dating from AD600, in which priests washed the feet of 12 poor people, just as Christ washed the feet of the Apostles.

◀ *Queen Elizabeth I performing the Maundy ceremonies, c.1565. By Teerlink, in the Beauchamp Collection, Devon.*

▶ *Her Majesty's Swan-Upping crew, led by the Royal Swanherd, on the River Thames.*

Swan-Upping

The mute swan has been a royal bird since at least the 12th century and, apart from those belonging to the two great City Livery Companies, the Dyers and the Vintners, all swans belong to the Crown. Every July the Companies' swan-herds meet the Royal Swanherd at Southwark Bridge and proceed up the Thames to Henley, catching and marking young swans. Each cygnet is marked like its parents: one nick on the beak for the Dyers' birds or two for the Vintners'. Unmarked birds belong to the Queen.

Doggett's Coat and Badge Race

This Thames watermen's race, now held on or near 1 August, was instituted in 1715 by Thomas Doggett, Irish actor and comedian, to mark the anniversary of George I's accession to the throne. At that time there were about 40,000 watermen working the Thames, which was the main highway in London. The 5-mile course, from Old London Bridge to Cadogan Pier, Chelsea, is no longer rowed against the tide and the old wherries have been replaced with racing skiffs. Nevertheless, the winner well deserves his prize: a scarlet coat, breeches and cap, white stockings and a silver badge bearing the White Horse of Hanover and the word 'Liberty'.

▲ Maundy purse and coins dating from the reign of George III.

▲ Past winners of Doggett's Coat and Badge Race in their scarlet costume.

▶ The silver badge awarded to the winner of Doggett's Coat and Badge Race.

Pomp and Circumstance

Trooping the Colour

The ceremony of Trooping the Colour at Horse Guards Parade, London, is one of the finest military parades in the world and, with a few breaks, has been carried out on The Sovereign's Official Birthday since 1805. It dates back to 1755 when an army's flag, or colour, was first trooped in front of soldiers so that they could recognize it as a rallying point in battle.

The Birthday Parade includes usually six Guards, each 73 strong, formed from the five Regiments of Foot Guards (Grenadier, Coldstream, Scots, Irish and Welsh Guards), The Household Cavalry (The Life Guards and The Blues and Royals) and some 350 musicians comprising the mounted bands of The Household Cavalry and the Massed Bands, Pipes and Drums of the Household Division.

The Sovereign, accompanied by an Escort of The Household Cavalry, arrives at the saluting base at 11am and, after inspecting the parade, watches as the Colour is trooped down the ranks. The Foot Guards then march past in slow and quick time, followed by The Household Cavalry, who walk and trot past. The Sovereign, at the head of the Guards, then returns down The Mall to Buckingham Palace for the final March Past.

Searching the Houses of Parliament

Before every State Opening of Parliament, the Yeomen of the Guard, resplendent in their scarlet and gold uniforms, assemble in the Prince's Chamber of the House of Lords. Ignoring the existence of electric light, they scrupulously search every nook and cranny of the cellars beneath the Palace of Westminster by the light of old candle-lanterns. When they are satisfied that all is well a message is sent to The Queen and Parliament is free to assemble.

▶ *The Yeomen of the Guard search the cellars of Westminster Palace.*

Pomp and Circumstance

Changing of the Guard, Whitehall

Whitehall Palace, the official Royal residence in Stuart times, was burned down in 1698 and Buckingham Palace did not become the official residence until Victoria acceded to the throne in 1837. She decreed that Horse Guards Arch should remain the official entrance to the Royal palaces and a Guard, provided alternately by The Life Guards and The Blues and Royals of The Household Cavalry, is still mounted daily. Every morning, the New Guard rides down The Mall to Whitehall where, with due ceremony, it replaces the Old Guard in the Front Yard or on Horse Guards.

◀ *Preparing for the daily Changing of the Guard at Whitehall, London.*

Ceremony of Her Majesty's Keys

For 700 years, the Tower of London has been secured each night by the Chief Yeoman Warder. Accompanied by the Escort to the Keys, he locks the gates of the Middle and Byward Towers before returning to the Bloody Tower Archway. Here, in response to the sentry's challenge, he utters the words 'Queen Elizabeth's Keys', to which the sentry replies 'Pass Queen Elizabeth's keys. All's well.' As the clock strikes ten, a bugler sounds the Last Post and the Chief Yeoman Warder then hands the keys into the care of the Resident Governor at The Queen's House.

▲ *The Ceremony of the Keys, Tower of London, 1898.*

◄ *Preparing to Beat the Bounds of the Tower of London, c.1900.*

The Tower Ravens
According to a superstition dating from the time of Charles II, when there are no longer ravens in the Tower of London, the White Tower will fall and a great disaster befall the Kingdom.

Beating the Bounds of the Tower of London

There are 31 numbered boundary marks around the Tower of London, starting at Tower Pier and continuing to the gate below Tower Bridge. Every three years, on Ascension Eve, a procession led by the Chief Yeoman Warder and including the choirboys of the Chapel Royal, the Resident Governor and Yeoman Warders sets out to beat the bounds. At each mark, the Tower Chaplain cries out 'Cursed is he who removeth his neighbour's land mark' and the Chief Yeoman Warder exhorts the choirboys to 'Whack it, boys! Whack it!', which they do with their willow wands.

Fire! Fire!

❖

Since 1605, when Parliament declared 5 November a
public holiday to celebrate the foiling of the Gunpowder
Plot, the ritual burning of effigies of Guy Fawkes on
bonfires has become the most widespread fire custom in
England. Much older are the pagan customs associated
with the turning points of the Celtic year: Midsummer;
Hallowe'en, when witches and the souls of the dead were
thought to be abroad; and New Year.

❖

▲ *People have danced round the Baal fire at Whalton each summer
for centuries.*

Midsummer Bonfires

The pre-Christian midsummer fires were intended to
strengthen the waning sun and a 14th-century monk noted
two types: bone fires to drive away evil and 'wake' fires, of
wood, which acted as a focal point for celebrations. At
Whalton, Northumberland, a huge bonfire is lit in the centre
of the village on Old Midsummer Eve (4 July), while chains
of midsummer fires can now be seen again in Cornwall.

Punkie Night

In late October, in Hinton St George, Somerset, the children carry
candle-lanterns made from hollowed-out mangold-wurzels through the
streets in the evening. This custom is associated with Hallowe'en, the
time when the dead were honoured and fires were lit for purification
and protection from evil, and the intricately carved lanterns
and their bearers represent the returning dead.

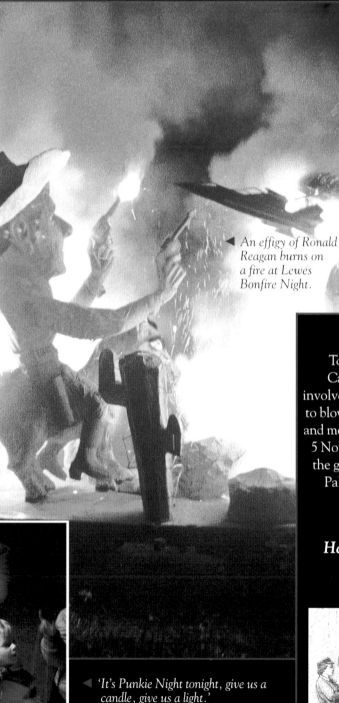

Lewes Bonfire Night

One of the most spectacular Guy Fawkes' celebrations can be seen at Lewes, in East Sussex, where bonfires, elaborately costumed parades and firework displays are organized by the various Bonfire Societies in the town and huge effigies of political and other figures are consigned to the flames. In fact, the first recorded bonfire night at Lewes was not held until 1679, when an effigy of the Pope was burned to commemorate the martyrdom of 17 Protestants burned as heretics during the reign of Mary I.

◄ *An effigy of Ronald Reagan burns on a fire at Lewes Bonfire Night.*

Guy Fawkes

Together with Robert Catesby and other Catholic conspirators, Guy Fawkes was involved in the infamous 1605 Gunpowder Plot to blow up the Protestant James I, his ministers and members of both Houses of Parliament. On 5 November, he was caught red-handed with the gunpowder in the cellars of Westminster Palace, then tortured, tried and hanged.

Guy, Guy, Guy,
String him up on high.
Hang him from a lamp-post and
and there let him die.

FOLK SONG

◄ *'It's Punkie Night tonight, give us a candle, give us a light.'*

► *'Remember, remember the fifth of November, gunpowder, treason and plot …'*

Fire! Fire!

Tar-Barrel Racing

Those seeking excitement with more than a hint of danger should visit Ottery St Mary, Devon, on the night of 5 November, where they will be greeted by the sight of a series of hogsheads of blazing tar being borne at full tilt along the road! Each bearer, with only sacking for protection, carries a barrel above his head as far as he can. Another man then takes over, and so on, until the barrel either becomes impossible to hold or falls apart. Teenagers and women also participate – they take their turn earlier in the day, using smaller barrels.

▶ *Tar-Barrel Racing at Ottery St Mary is one of the most alarming customs in the country.*

▼ *The Stonehaven custom of Swinging the Fireballs is not as dangerous as it looks.*

Swinging the Fireballs

At Stonehaven, the Old Year is burned out with fireballs – wire-netting baskets full of tar-soaked combustible materials attached by a length of stout wire to a handle. These are lit on the stroke of midnight on New Year's Eve. The young men then parade along the main street of the old town, whirling the fireballs around their heads in great fiery arcs.

Burning the Clavie

In this ancient New Year fire ritual from Burghead, the Clavie – an 'archangel' whisky barrel full of blazing wood, set on a salmon-fisher's stake – is carried around the boundaries of the old town by the 'Clavie Crew', who pause to present lucky smouldering faggots to various householders. At Doorie Hill, the Clavie is set into an altar-like stone, where it burns until the Crew set about it with a hatchet, scattering flaming fragments to the crowd.

▶ *Burning the Clavie is one of several ancient New Year fire rituals.*

▼ *The burning of the longship is the climax of the Up-Helly-Aa celebrations at Lerwick, in the Shetlands.*

Up-Helly-Aa

In late January, to celebrate the end of Old Yule, a full-sized replica of a Norse galley is dragged through Lerwick, escorted by Guizers dressed as Vikings and led by Guizer Jarl, and a host of other Guizers clad in fantastic costumes and carrying blazing torches. At the Burning Site, the torches are flung into the galley and, as the flames leap, 'The Norseman's Home' is sung and all the ships in the harbour sound their sirens. This dramatic commemoration of the 600 years when the Shetlands and Orkneys were subject to the Norse crown has developed since the far more dangerous practice of racing tar-barrels on sledges through the streets was banned in the 1880s!

High Days and Holidays

❖

Shrovetide and Easter, which mark the beginning and end of Lent, are traditionally seasons for a variety of lively and energetic games, perhaps to compensate for the austerity of the Lenten fast. Of the various ball-games played at these times, the anarchic street football is probably the most widespread. Not surprisingly, pancakes – which were a convenient way of using up butter and fats before the fast – and Easter eggs – ancient symbol of renewal of life – feature in other games.

❖

Pancake Racing

Tossing pancakes, especially while running, makes for great sport and the Shrove Tuesday pancake race at Olney is nationally famous. The women of Olney and nearby Warmington don aprons and headscarves for the occasion and, armed with pancakes and frying pans, assemble in the village square. From here they race for some 400 metres to the parish church, tossing their pancakes three times on the way. The winner receives a prayerbook, after which all the frying pans are laid around the church and a service of blessing is held.

▼ *The Shrove Tuesday Pancake Race has been held in Olney, Buckinghamshire, since the mid-15th century.*

A kiss for a woman,
A cake for a man,
Run to the church
With a frying pan.

CHILDREN'S RHYME

Skipping

In Scarborough, at the ringing of the Pancake Bell on Shrove Tuesday, everyone assembles on the promenade to skip. Long ropes are stretched across the road and there may be ten or more people skipping on one rope. The origins of this custom are obscure but skipping was once a magical game, associated with the sowing and sprouting of seeds, which may well have been played on barrows (burial mounds) during the Middle Ages.

◄ *Shrovetide skipping on the promenade at Scarborough, North Yorkshire.*

▲ *Specially painted balls are used for the Shrovetide football at Ashbourne in Derbyshire.*

Street Football

Because it has no precise rules and, more importantly, no precise number of players, street football is a game in which anyone brave enough can join. Most games are between two teams hailing from either different parts of the town or neighbouring parishes; the Eastertide football at Workington, for example, is between the 'Downies' from the harbour area and the 'Uppies' from the castle a mile or so away. The goals, if there are any, may be miles apart and, in some cases, it is sufficient to get the ball back onto home ground to score.

► *The Eastertide football between the 'Uppies' and 'Downies' of Workington is a formidable contest.*

High Days and Holidays

Easter-Egg Customs

The original Easter eggs were hard-boiled eggs, stained with vegetable dyes, and often elaborately decorated. The custom of rolling Easter eggs downhill is observed every Easter Monday at Avenham Park, Preston, in Lancashire, although chocolate eggs, or even oranges, tend to be used nowadays. Somewhat reminiscent of 'conkers' is the northern game of 'jauping' (Scottish for 'splattering'), in which each player holds an egg and strikes in turn at the other's egg until one breaks.

► *The practice of colouring and decorating hard-boiled eggs for Easter is widespread throughout Europe.*

▲ *Easter-egg rolling on Easter Monday at Avenham Park, Preston, Lancashire.*

The Easter Hare

The hare was sacred to the Anglo-Saxon goddess Eostre, from whose name we get the word 'Easter', and throughout Europe, the hare is the traditional bringer of Easter eggs. On the darker side, witches were widely thought to transform themselves into hares. The transformation of the hare into the 'Easter Bunny' may have resulted from a natural confusion between the two animals or a wish to disguise its pagan origins.

Hare-Pie Scramble and Bottle-Kicking

This two-part custom takes place each Easter Monday at Hallaton, Leicestershire. The hare-pie is all that remains of a form of rent exacted from the incumbent clergyman in medieval times. The pie was once cut up and scattered over Hare-Pie Bank, to be scrambled for by the villagers, but is nowadays more likely to be distributed at the church-gate by the rector. The bottle-kicking, between the villages of Hallaton and Medbourne, takes place at the Bank, although the bottles are small wooden barrels – two full of ale and one dummy – and there is no actual kicking. The object is to wrest each bottle away from the Bank and over the home boundary.

◀ *Hare-Pie Scramble and Bottle-Kicking, Hallaton.*

Cheese-Rolling

Rolling cheeses is infinitely more dangerous than rolling eggs, especially when the cheeses are 7lb (3.5kg) Double Gloucesters tumbling down Cooper's Hill. This hair-raising affair, which formerly took place on Whit Monday, is presided over by a Master of Ceremonies, resplendent in white coat and beribboned hat. In each of four races, a cheese is sent rolling down the hill and the contestants rush after it, the first to the bottom being the winner. This custom is probably a relic of a 500-year-old ceremony associated with grazing rights in the village of Brockworth.

▼ *The annual Cheese-Rolling at Cooper's Hill, in Gloucestershire is not without its casualties.*

Many customs have arisen as a result of conditions left in wills or other legal documents. Centuries ago, when poverty was common-place, local dignitaries often made bequests to benefit the poor of their parish and, over the years, these have become established customs, albeit in a slightly different form.

Cakes and Ale

> ▶ The Fenny Poppers at Fenny Stratford are fired at intervals throughout St Martin's Day.

Pax Cakes

In 1570, to encourage good neighbourliness among parishioners, Lady Scudamore arranged for five shillingsworth of cake and ninepenn'orth of ale to be provided every Palm Sunday in four Herefordshire churches. Nowadays, small biscuits stamped with the image of the Pascal lamb and the words 'God and Good Neighbourhood' are distributed at the church doors after the service.

◀ Pax Cakes are distributed every year on Palm Sunday.

Tuppenny Starvers

Thanks to a bequest made in 1739, children attending morning service at St Michael's Church, Bristol, on Easter Tuesday are given enormous spicy buns. At the time of the bequest, tuppenny buns, intended for the choirboys, were a special treat compared with the more usual penny ones.

◀ Bristol children who are given a Tuppenny Starver certainly need a very good appetite!

Firing the Fenny Poppers

When Dr Willis Browne founded St Martin's Church, Fenny Stratford, in 1730, he arranged for a feast to be held each St Martin's Day (11 November). After his death, the parishioners decided to enhance the occasion by firing the old cannons which the doctor had presented to the church. The current 'Fenny Poppers' are six cast-iron pots, which are loaded with gunpowder and fired in rapid succession at intervals throughout the day.

◄ *The collection of buns in The Widow's Son public house has been accumulating for over a century.*

The Widow's Bun

In London's East End, as a condition of the lease, a hot-cross bun must be hung up in The Widow's Son public house by a serving sailor every Easter. This poignant custom commemorates a local widow who saved a hot-cross bun each year for her sailor son, although he never returned from sea.

The Mystery Plays

These medieval plays were travelling re-enactments of Bible stories, performed by city tradesmen's guilds. Stories were allocated appropriately by the city authorities, eg the Flood might be assigned to the Water-Drawers and the Last Supper to the Bakers, and the plays were staged on wheeled 'pageant-wagons'. The four surviving collections of these plays – in Chester, Coventry, Wakefield and York – are performed in certain years.

◄ *A scene from the Chester Mystery Play: The Flood.*

Calendar of Selected Customs

These dates are subject to change, or the events may even be cancelled altogether, so it is advisable to consult the local Tourist Information Centre or local newspapers beforehand.

JANUARY

c.11th (*Old New Year's Eve*) — Burning the Clavie, Burghead, Highland, Scotland.

c. 29th (*End of Old Yule*) — Up-Helly-Aa, Lerwick, Shetland Isles.

MOVABLE FEASTS

Shrove Tuesday — Pancake Race, Olney, Buckinghamshire.
Skipping, Scarborough, North Yorkshire.
Football, Ashbourne, Derbyshire.

Palm Sunday — Pax Cakes at Hentland, Hoarwithy, King's Caple and Sellack, in present-day Hereford and Worcester.

Maundy Thursday — Royal Maundy, various cathedrals.

Good Friday — Widow's Bun, The Widow's Son, Devons Road, Bromley-by-Bow, London.
Mumming Play (Midgeley Pace-Eggers), Calder Valley, West Yorkshire.
Football, Workington, Cumbria.

Easter Saturday — Britannia Coconut Dancers, Bacup, Lancashire.

Easter Monday — Hare-Pie Scramble and Bottle-Kicking, Hallaton, Leicestershire.
Easter-egg rolling, Avenham Park, Preston, Lancashire.

Easter Tuesday — Tuppenny Starvers, St Michael-on-the-Mount Without, Bristol, Avon.
Football, Workington, Cumbria.

Ascensiontide — Well-Dressing, Tissington, Derbyshire.

MAY

1st (*May Day*) — 'Obby 'Oss Day, Padstow, Cornwall.
Sailor's Horse, Minehead, Somerset.
Singing, Magdalen Tower, Oxford.

First Sunday — Clootie Wells, Munlochy Bay, Grampian, Scotland.

c. 8th (*St Michael's Day*) — Furry Dance, Helston, Cornwall.

13th (*Old May Day*) — Garland Day, Abbotsbury, Dorset.

29th (*Oak Apple Day*) — Grovely Day, Great Wishford, Wiltshire.

Spring Bank Holiday — Cheese-Rolling, Cooper's Hill, near Brockworth, Gloucestershire.

JUNE

23rd (*Midsummer Eve*) — Midsummer bonfires, Cornwall.

c. 24th (*Midsummer Day*) — Well-Dressing, Youlgreave, Derbyshire.
Well-Dressing, Tideswell, Derbyshire.

JULY

c. 4th (*Old Midsummer Eve*) — Baal Fire, Whalton, Northumberland.

End July — Swan-Upping, River Thames, London–Henley.

AUGUST

c. 1st — Doggett's Coat and Badge Race, River Thames, London.

OCTOBER

Last Thursday — Punkie Night, Hinton St George, Somerset.

c. 30th — Mumming Play (Antobus Soulers), Antrobus, Cheshire.

NOVEMBER

5th (*Guy Fawkes Day*) — Bonfire Night, Lewes, East Sussex.
Tar-Barrel Racing, Ottery St Mary, Devon.

11th (*St Martin's Day*) — Firing the Fenny Poppers, Fenny Stratford, Buckinghamshire.

DECEMBER

26th (*Boxing Day*) — Mumming Play, Marshfield, Avon.
Mumming Play, Symondsbury, Dorset.

31st (*New Year's Eve*) — Swinging the Fireballs, Stonehaven, Grampian.

DAILY OR OCCASIONAL

Daily — Changing of the Guard, Whitehall, London.
Nightly Ceremony of the Keys, Tower of London.
Ripon Hornblower, Ripon, North Yorkshire.

Before State Opening of Parliament — Searching the Houses of Parliament, London.

ANNUAL

Trooping the Colour, London.

EVERY THREE YEARS

Beating the Bounds, Tower of London (next in 2002).
Mystery plays: Chester, Coventry, Wakefield, York.